The Art of Affiliate Marketing: Leveraging Digital Partnerships for Profit in 2023

Table of Contents

Introduction

Welcome to "The Art of Affiliate Marketing." This book is designed to provide you with an in-depth understanding of the lucrative world of affiliate marketing. Whether you're a beginner who's just starting or a seasoned pro looking for new strategies, this book will serve as your guide.

Chapter 1: Understanding Affiliate Marketing

Affiliate marketing is a revenue-sharing venture between a website owner and an online merchant. The website owner places advertisements on their site to help sell the merchant's products or to send potential customers to the merchant's website. In return, they receive a share of the profits.

Chapter 2: The Power of Partnerships: Affiliate Networks

Affiliate networks serve as intermediaries between merchants (brands) that sell products or services and the affiliates (publishers) that promote them. We delve into the role and importance of these networks, and how to choose the right one for your affiliate business.

Chapter 3: Choosing Your Niche

Your chosen niche will play a huge role in your success as an affiliate marketer. This chapter explores the process of selecting the right niche, which aligns with your interests, has profitable potential, and offers sufficient market demand.

Chapter 4: Setting Up Your Affiliate Marketing Business

In this chapter, we cover the technical aspects of setting up your affiliate marketing business. From choosing the right platform and domain name to creating compelling content and integrating affiliate links.

Chapter 5: SEO and Content Marketing for Affiliates

To attract traffic and build an audience, affiliate marketers must understand the principles of SEO and content marketing. This chapter outlines these concepts and provides actionable strategies to apply them to your affiliate marketing business.

Chapter 6: Email Marketing: Your Secret Weapon

Email marketing remains one of the most effective marketing channels for building trust and driving conversions. Here we dive into the importance of building an email list, crafting effective email campaigns, and best practices for email marketing in an affiliate context.

Chapter 7: Social Media and Influencer Marketing

In the era of Instagram, YouTube, TikTok, and other platforms, leveraging social media and influencer marketing can significantly boost your affiliate marketing success. This chapter explores various strategies to harness the power of these platforms.

Chapter 8: Leveraging PPC Advertising for Affiliate Marketing

PPC (pay-per-click) advertising is a valuable strategy for driving targeted traffic to your affiliate offers. This chapter explains how PPC works, how to set up your campaigns, and how to optimize them for maximum ROI.

Chapter 9: Data Analytics: Measuring Your Success

Data is essential in understanding your business performance and making informed decisions. We will discuss key metrics to track, how to interpret your data, and use it to optimize your strategies.

Chapter 10: Legal and Ethical Considerations

This chapter will help you understand the legal aspects of affiliate marketing, including disclosure requirements and privacy regulations, to ensure your business is compliant.

Conclusion

In conclusion, we will revisit key concepts, offer some final thoughts and inspiration, and provide resources for continuous learning in the field of affiliate marketing. You will be equipped with the knowledge and tools to navigate this exciting and profitable world of digital marketing.

Please note, the information provided in each chapter is meant to be comprehensive yet easily understandable. Whether you're just starting your affiliate marketing journey or have already embarked on it, this book aims to enhance your knowledge, refine your strategies, and amplify your success in this industry.

Each chapter will also include practical exercises, real-world examples, and actionable tips to help you apply what you have learned and see tangible results in your affiliate marketing efforts.

So, let's embark on this journey together to uncover the art and science of affiliate marketing. The world of digital entrepreneurship awaits you.

Author's Note

Affiliate marketing is an exciting journey that requires a constant hunger for learning and an unyielding dedication to your business. While it may seem daunting at first, remember that every successful affiliate marketer started where you are now. Your potential for success is limitless.

Stay patient, persistent, and always remember to provide genuine value to your audience. Success in affiliate marketing, like any business, does not come overnight but is the product of consistent effort, strategic planning, and an unwavering commitment to your audience.

Let's dive in and discover the potential of affiliate marketing together!

Chapter 1

Understanding Affiliate Marketing

Affiliate marketing is a digital strategy where businesses (merchants) partner with individuals or other businesses (affiliates) to promote their products or services. Affiliates earn a commission for every purchase or specific action (like a sign-up or click) that occurs as a result of traffic they direct to the merchant's site.

Affiliate marketing operates on a revenue-sharing model, presenting a win-win situation for both the merchant and the affiliate. The merchant benefits from increased sales or leads and brand visibility, while the affiliate earns passive income.

The Players: Merchants, Affiliates, and Consumers

Merchants (Advertisers)

Merchants (also referred to as advertisers or vendors) are the creators or providers of a product or service, from multinational corporations and small businesses to individuals who sell something on eBay or Etsy. Merchants set the terms of an affiliate program, such as its commission structure.

Affiliates (Publishers)

Affiliates (also referred to as publishers) are individuals or businesses who promote products or services sold by merchants on a wide variety of platforms such as blogs, social media profiles or email lists. Affiliates use these platforms to drive visitors directly to merchant's sites through unique affiliate links provided.

Consumers (Customers)

Consumers are the driving force behind affiliate marketing. They are the ones who click on the affiliate's links and make a purchase. Without consumers, there are no sales, and without sales, there's no commission for the affiliate and no revenue for the merchant.

How It Works

1. Affiliates promote products/services: Affiliates promote the merchant's products or services on their platform using unique affiliate links provided by the merchant or affiliate network.
2. Consumer clicks on the affiliate link: The consumer, enticed by the affiliate's promotional efforts, clicks on the unique affiliate link, which contains a tracking code.
3. The affiliate's ID is stored in a cookie: Once the consumer clicks on the affiliate link, a cookie gets stored in their browser. This cookie contains the affiliate's unique ID and tracks the visitor's actions.
4. Consumer makes a purchase: The consumer proceeds to make a purchase on the merchant's site.
5. Sale gets tracked: The merchant tracks the purchase and attributes it to the right affiliate through the cookie's stored ID.
6. Affiliate earns a commission: Once the purchase is confirmed, the merchant pays the affiliate a percentage of the sale as a commission.

Types of Affiliate Marketing Models

Affiliate marketing operates under different models, each offering a unique approach to earning revenue:

1. Pay Per Sale (PPS): The affiliate earns a commission whenever the consumer makes a purchase through their affiliate link. This is the most common type of affiliate marketing.

2. Pay Per Click (PPC): The affiliate earns money whenever a consumer clicks on their affiliate links and is redirected to the merchant's website. The affiliate gets paid for driving traffic, regardless of whether a sale occurs.

3. Pay Per Lead (PPL): The affiliate gets paid for every lead they generate. This could be a form fill-up, a free trial sign-up, a subscription, or any other agreed-upon action that doesn't necessarily involve a direct purchase.

In the following chapter, we'll delve deeper into affiliate networks - key intermediaries in affiliate marketing that facilitate successful partnerships and smooth transactions between merchants and affiliates.

Chapter 2

The Power of Partnerships: Affiliate Networks

After you understand the basic tenets of affiliate marketing, the next step should be exploring partnership opportunities facilitated by affiliate networks.

What are Affiliate Networks?

An affiliate network acts as an intermediary between merchants (brands) and affiliates (publishers). Essentially, they provide a platform where merchants list their products, and affiliates choose which ones they want to promote. They also handle tracking, reporting, and payment processes.

The Role of Affiliate Networks

Affiliate networks play a significant role in the affiliate marketing landscape. They provide several benefits to both merchants and affiliates.

For Merchants:

Reach: Affiliate networks give merchants access to a vast pool of affiliates, significantly increasing their products' reach.

2. Time and Resource Management: Affiliate networks handle the tracking of sales, clicks, and leads. They also manage the payment of affiliate commissions, saving merchants considerable time and resources.
3. Trust and Credibility: Working with a reputable affiliate network adds credibility to a merchant's affiliate program, making it more attractive to potential affiliates.

For Affiliates:

1. Opportunity: Affiliate networks provide affiliates with access to a wide variety of merchants and products, offering numerous opportunities to find a program that fits their niche and audience.
2. Simplicity: With tracking, reporting, and payments centralized within the affiliate network, affiliates can manage all their partnerships in one place.
3. Reliability: Affiliates can trust that they will be paid for their efforts on time and in full, thanks to the reliability of established affiliate networks.

Choosing the Right Affiliate Network

With many affiliate networks to choose from, it's crucial to pick one that aligns with your goals, niche, and audience. Here are some factors to consider:

1. Reputation: Look for networks that are reliable and well-regarded in the industry.
2. Variety of Merchants and Products: Look for a network that has a good mix of merchants and products, especially those that fit your niche and audience.
3. Payment Structure and Frequency: Understand the network's payment terms. How often are payments made? What's the payment threshold? Are there different payment methods available?

4. Support: A good affiliate network provides excellent customer support to its affiliates.
5. Tools and Resources: Check if the network offers tools for tracking performance and resources for learning and growth.

Some Popular Affiliate Networks

To give you a head start, here are a few well-regarded affiliate networks in the industry:

1. Amazon Associates: Amazon's affiliate program gives you access to a vast array of products. It's an excellent choice for beginners due to its ease of use.
2. ClickBank: Known for digital products and online courses, ClickBank offers high commission rates.
3. Commission Junction (CJ): This network has a vast selection of big-name brands and offers robust reporting tools.
4. ShareASale: With a mix of both physical and digital products across various niches, ShareASale is a favorite among many affiliates.
5. Rakuten Affiliate Network: Formerly known as LinkShare, Rakuten is a well-established network with a broad mix of advertisers.

Remember, while the power of partnerships can significantly enhance your affiliate marketing business, the choice of network should align with your individual goals and audience needs.

In the next chapter, we'll dive into one of the most critical aspects of affiliate marketing: choosing your niche.

Chapter 3

Choosing Your Niche

Selecting your niche is one of the key steps in beginning an affiliate marketing journey. Your niche will determine your target audience, the products you promote and the type of content you produce - it is therefore essential to choose one that aligns with your passions and interests, has a viable market and contains products you can sell as an affiliate marketer.

What is a Niche?

Marketing-wise, the term "niche" refers to any specialized segment of a market; an area of specialization or interest. As an affiliate marketer, your niche could include anything from organic skincare products and fitness equipment to DIY crafts and digital marketing tools - whatever suits you best and your target customers best!

Why is Choosing a Niche Important?

Focusing on one niche allows you to reach a targeted audience with specific needs and interests, building expertise in that area and earning trust among your target market while making your affiliate marketing more effective.

Steps to Choosing Your Niche

Step 1: Identify Your Interests and Passions

Starting with something you're passionate about makes the journey more enjoyable and sustainable. Write down topics you're interested in and have good knowledge about.

Step 2: Conduct Market Research

Once you have a list of potential niches, it's time to conduct market research. This involves checking the demand for your potential niches, the competition, and the availability of affiliate products. You can use tools like Google Trends, Keyword Planner, and SEMRush for this research.

Step 3: Evaluate Monetization Potential

Not all niches are profitable. You need to check if there are affiliate products available in your chosen niche. Browse through affiliate networks to see if there are products that align with your niche.

Step 4: Check the Competition

A good niche will have a moderate level of competition. Too little competition might indicate a lack of demand, while too much competition could make it challenging to gain traction.

Step 5: Make a Decision

Based on your findings, choose a niche that aligns with your interests, has sufficient market demand, profitable potential, and a moderate level of competition.

Examples of Profitable Niches

Here are a few examples of profitable niches in affiliate marketing:

1. Health and Wellness: This niche covers a broad range of topics from dietary supplements to fitness equipment and mental health resources.
2. Finance: Products in this niche can range from investing guides to budgeting tools and online courses about financial planning.
3. Home Decor and DIY: From furniture to home improvement tools, this niche appeals to the vast number of people interested in home aesthetics and DIY projects.
4. Technology and Gadgets: Tech enthusiasts are always on the lookout for the latest devices, making this a profitable niche.
5. Online Learning/Education: With the rise of online learning, promoting online courses or learning tools can be lucrative.

At its core, an ideal niche will combine your interests, knowledge and the needs of your target audience. In the next chapter we'll look at how to set up an affiliate marketing business once you have chosen your niche.

Chapter 4

Setting Up Your Affiliate Marketing Business

Once you have identified your niche, the next step in affiliate marketing business setup involves setting up a platform where you will promote affiliate products, building your online presence, and setting up essential business systems.

Step 1: Building Your Platform

Option 1: Start a Blog or Website

Blogs or websites are the preferred platform for affiliate marketing. By having a blog, it enables you to produce content around your chosen niche, add affiliate links and grow an audience. WordPress is often chosen due to its ease of use, flexibility and abundance of helpful plugins that enable beginners to start marketing themselves successfully online.

Option 2: Use Social Media

If you already have a strong following on social media, this could be a great place to start your affiliate marketing journey. Each social media platform has different strengths, so you'll want to choose one that aligns with your niche and target audience. For example, Instagram and Pinterest are great for niches that rely heavily on visuals, while LinkedIn could be a great platform for a B2B niche.

Option 3: Email Marketing

Email lists can be an effective asset in affiliate marketing, providing your audience with invaluable content delivered directly into their inboxes and helping build strong relationships while more efficiently marketing affiliate products.

Step 2: Content Creation

Once you've chosen your platform, you'll need to create content around your niche. Your content should be valuable to your audience and should subtly include your affiliate links. Remember, the primary aim is to provide value; the promotion is secondary.

Step 3: Search Engine Optimization (SEO)

SEO (Search Engine Optimization) is critical in making sure that more people view your content, leading to more traffic on websites or blogs. By optimizing it for search engines, your content will gain increased exposure in search results resulting in greater visits for your website or blog.

Step 4: Building an Audience

Building an audience requires time and dedication. You must promote your content, interact with users and deliver value consistently in order to establish trust among your followers. Over time, they'll come to depend on you as their resource!

Step 5: Joining Affiliate Programs

Once your platform is in place, it's time to join affiliate programs. Be sure to choose ones that resonate with your niche and audience - take your time researching all possible programs while considering factors like commission rate, product quality, brand reputation and support services before selecting an affiliate partner.

Step 6: Promotion

Now, you're ready to start promoting products. Include your affiliate links in your content and start driving traffic to the merchant's site.

Step 7: Monitoring and Adjusting Your Strategies

Affiliate marketing requires continuous learning and adjustment. Monitor your results, see what's working and what's not, and adjust your strategies accordingly.

Setting up your affiliate marketing business is a significant step towards creating a passive income stream. However, remember that success won't happen overnight. Be patient, stay consistent, and keep learning. In the next chapter, we'll discuss content creation in more detail, providing you with strategies to create engaging content that promotes your affiliate products effectively

Chapter 5

Mastering the Art of Content Creation

Content is at the heart of affiliate marketing. It's through content that you provide value to your audience, establish trust, and subtly promote your affiliate products. But not all content is created equal. In this chapter, we'll explore how to create engaging, high-quality content that resonates with your audience and drives conversions.

Understanding Your Audience

Before creating content, it's essential that you fully comprehend your target audience. Who are they, their interests, challenges and desires; which forms of media are consumed most by this demographic and where? Answering such queries will enable you to produce work which resonates with its target demographic.

Types of Content

There are many types of content you can create as an affiliate marketer. Here are a few examples:

Blog Posts

Blog posts are an essential form of content in affiliate marketing, offering an ideal medium for in-depth discussions, reviews and tutorials.

Social Media Posts

Social media offers a more casual and interactive platform for promoting your affiliate products. Depending on the platform you can post various types of posts ranging from text/image posts, videos/stories etc.

Videos

Videos are a powerful tool for affiliate marketing. You can create product reviews, tutorials, unboxing videos, and more. Platforms like YouTube are perfect for video content.

Email Newsletters

Email newsletters offer an easy and engaging way for you to communicate directly with your target audience. They allow you to provide exclusive content, share updates and promote affiliate products more directly.

Creating High-Quality Content

Creating high-quality content involves more than just stringing words together. Here are some tips:

Provide Value

Your content should provide value to your audience in some form or another - be it solving an issue, imparting new information or entertaining. Doing this builds trust with them and increases the chance that they'll click on one of your affiliate links.

Be Authentic

Promote products that you've used, tested, or thoroughly researched. This way, you can share honest opinions and experiences, which adds credibility to your content.

Make Your Content Engaging

Find ways to make your content engaging - this could include storytelling, visuals, interactive elements or simply using a conversational tone.

Include a Call to Action (CTA)

Always include a clear CTA in your content. This could be prompting your audience to click on an affiliate link, leave a comment, share your content, or subscribe to your newsletter.

SEO Best Practices

Optimizing your content for search engines increases its visibility and helps you attract more organic traffic. Here are some SEO best practices:

Use Keywords

Identify the keywords that your target audience uses to search for content in your niche. Incorporate these keywords naturally in your content, especially in your titles, headings, and meta descriptions.

Optimize Your Images

When using images in your content, make sure they're optimized by choosing relevant file names, decreasing file sizes for increased page load speed, and using alt tags to describe each one.

Build Backlinks

Backlinks are links from other websites to your content. They're seen as a vote of confidence by search engines and can significantly improve your SEO. You can build backlinks by creating high-quality content, guest posting on other websites, and building relationships with other creators in your niche.

Mastering content creation takes time and practice. Be mindful to place your audience first in all content you create; strive to deliver value with each creation process and strive to add something of benefit. In our next chapter we'll also cover strategies to promote affiliate products more effectively and increase conversion rates.

Chapter 6

Strategies to Promote Your Affiliate Products

After selecting your niche and creating high-quality content for affiliate products, the next crucial step should be promoting them effectively to drive conversions and maximize earnings. In this chapter you'll learn various tactics designed to boost conversion rates while increasing earnings.

1. Product Reviews

One of the most effective ways to promote affiliate products is by writing detailed, honest product reviews. Share your experiences, the pros and cons, and who might benefit most from the product. High-quality images or a video demonstration can enhance your reviews, making them more helpful and engaging for your audience

2. Tutorials and How-to Guides

Tutorials and how-to guides that incorporate affiliate products can be immensely effective. For instance, in the beauty niche, offering step-by-step makeup tutorials using certain items can encourage viewers to purchase those products.

3. Email Marketing

As mentioned earlier, email marketing offers a more personal way to reach your audience. Use your emails to share valuable content, offer exclusive deals, or highlight particular products. Remember to maintain a balance between providing value and promoting products.

4. Social Media Promotion

Social media platforms offer numerous avenues to promote your affiliate products. This could involve regular posts, stories, live videos or paid advertisements - just be sure to comply with each platform's rules on affiliate marketing in order to avoid any problems!

5. Webinars or Live Streams

Hosting webinars or live streams is an engaging and effective way to interact with your target audience, provide detailed information, and promote affiliate products. For instance, hosting one could teach attendees specific skills while suggesting products which would assist them with better practicing that skill more efficiently.

6. Banners and Widgets

Many affiliate programs provide banners, widgets, and other promotional materials that you can easily incorporate into your website. However, be mindful of not cluttering your website with too many banners as it may distract and turn off your readers.

7. Discounts and Special Offers

If your affiliate program allows it, offering exclusive discounts or special offers can incentivize your audience to purchase through your affiliate link.

8. SEO

While not a direct promotion strategy, optimizing your content for search engines is a long-term strategy that can significantly boost your organic traffic and increase the visibility of your affiliate promotions.

Be Ethical and Transparent

As you promote your affiliate products, remember to always be ethical and transparent. This includes disclosing your affiliate relationships to your audience and promoting products responsibly. Trust is a vital component of affiliate marketing, and maintaining your audience's trust should always be a priority.

Remember, what works well for one person or audience may not work so well for others. Test different strategies, track your results, and keep refining your approach until it meets both you and your target audience's needs best. In our next chapter, we will look into expanding and scaling up your affiliate marketing business for greater success.

Chapter 7

Scaling Your Affiliate Marketing Business

Once your affiliate marketing business starts gaining traction, it's time to think about scaling. Scaling involves taking what works and doing more of it, refining your strategies, and leveraging additional tools and resources to increase your earnings. Here are some strategies for scaling your affiliate marketing business:

Diversify Your Affiliate Products

Promoting a wider variety of products can help you reach a larger audience and increase your earning potential. Just make sure any new products you promote are still relevant to your niche and valuable to your audience.

Leverage Paid Advertising

While organic strategies are essential for sustainable, long-term growth, paid advertising can boost your visibility and conversions in the short term. Consider using pay-per-click advertising on platforms like Google AdWords or social media advertising on platforms like Facebook or Instagram.

Explore Other Affiliate Programs

Joining additional affiliate programs can provide new earning opportunities. Different programs offer different commission rates, promotional materials, and support, so diversifying your programs can help you find what works best for you.

Expand Your Content Types and Channels

If you are only creating one type of content or using one platform, consider expanding. If you're only writing blog posts, why not experiment with creating videos? Or, if Instagram is all that's used currently, perhaps branching out onto YouTube or Pinterest as well?

Automate and Outsource

As your business expands, it may become apparent that certain tasks could be automated or outsourced more easily. For instance, using email marketing software to automate newsletters would save time while hiring a virtual assistant could assist with managing social media pages.

Focus on Building Your Email List

Your email list is an invaluable asset that allows you to connect directly with your audience. By offering informative content and cultivating strong relationships, your list can increase conversions while expanding business growth.

Stay Current with Industry Trends and Best Practices

The world of affiliate marketing is always evolving. By staying up-to-date with the latest trends and best practices, you can ensure your strategies remain effective and take advantage of new opportunities.

Scaling your affiliate marketing business requires careful planning and strategic decision-making. It's important to remember that scaling doesn't always mean getting bigger - it also means becoming more efficient and effective. By focusing on what works, refining your strategies, and leveraging the right tools and resources, you can increase your earnings while maintaining - or even improving - the quality of your work. In the next chapter, we'll discuss how to maintain your affiliate marketing business for long-term success.

Chapter 8

Maintaining Your Affiliate Marketing Business for Long-term Success

As with any business, maintaining an affiliate marketing business is just as essential to its long-term viability as starting one. Our aim here is to establish sustainable sources of income; in this chapter we'll go through various strategies to keep it thriving for years.

Consistently Deliver High-Quality Content

The importance of delivering high-quality content to your audience cannot be overstated. This doesn't only mean the actual written or visual content but also the products you're promoting. Make sure the products you associate yourself with continue to be of high quality and relevance to your audience.

Engage With Your Audience

Relationships you form with your audience will be key to long-term success. Keep engaging with them by replying to comments, emails or messages they send your way, asking their opinion and showing your gratitude for their support.

Keep Up With SEO Trends

Search engine algorithms evolve constantly, so to ensure that your content continues to rank well on search engines you must keep up. Learn about the latest SEO practices and update both content and strategies as necessary.

Stay Updated With Your Affiliate Programs

Stay informed on changes in your affiliate programs, whether they involve commission structures, product offerings or policies that could impact earnings or how to promote products. It is vital that you remain up-to-date.

Regularly Review and Update Your Content

Over time, some of your content may become outdated. To maintain relevance, it's essential that you review it regularly and update as necessary - whether this involves updating a blog post with more current information, upgrading an affiliate product to one with updated specifications, or revamping SEO strategies.

Regularly Analyze Your Performance

Use analytics tools to regularly review your performance. Which strategies are working well, and which aren't? What type of content does your audience engage with the most? Use these insights to refine your strategies and focus on what works best.

Diversify Your Income Streams

Relying solely on affiliate marketing could be risky. Diversifying your income streams can provide financial stability. This could involve creating your own products, offering services, or exploring other types of online marketing.

Keep Learning and Adapting

Digital marketing is ever-evolving, presenting new platforms, trends, and strategies every year. By staying abreast of these changes and adapting accordingly, you can keep pace with industry developments while seizing any emerging opportunities that present themselves.

Maintaining an affiliate marketing business takes dedication, engagement and adaptation - but with commitment, engagement with audiences, the delivery of high-quality content, constant learning and adaptation you can build a sustainable affiliate marketing business. In our next chapter we will cover some common pitfalls to be wary of when engaging in affiliate marketing.

Chapter 9

Common Pitfalls to Avoid in Affiliate Marketing

While affiliate marketing can provide a significant source of income when done right, there are several common pitfalls that new affiliate marketers often fall into. Being aware of these can save you from making costly mistakes and ensure your affiliate marketing journey is as smooth as possible.

Pitfall 1: Promoting Low-Quality Products

While it can be tempting to promote any product with an attractive commission rate, low-quality offerings could damage both your reputation and that of your audience. Always ensure any item promoted is high-quality and truly beneficial to them.

Pitfall 2: Not Disclosing Affiliate Links

Not only is disclosing affiliate links a legal requirement in many regions, but it's also an important aspect of building trust with your audience. Be transparent about your affiliate links to maintain trust and stay compliant with regulations.

Pitfall 3: Ignoring SEO

Misusing SEO can severely limit the reach of your content. Without optimization, search engine results might not rank it highly and make it harder for readers to discover you.

Pitfall 4: Expecting Immediate Success

Affiliate marketing is not a get-rich-quick scheme. It takes time to build an audience, establish trust, and start earning significant commissions. Be patient, stay consistent, and keep focusing on providing value to your audience.

Pitfall 5: Failing to Understand Your Audience

Understanding your audience is of utmost importance in affiliate marketing. Without an understanding of their needs, interests, and challenges you cannot create content that resonates with them or promote products they will find worthwhile.

Pitfall 6: Overloading Your Content with Affiliate Links

While it's essential to include affiliate links in your content, overdoing it can harm your credibility and your SEO. Ensure your content is primarily focused on providing value, with affiliate links naturally incorporated.

Pitfall 7: Neglecting Email Marketing

Failing to build an email list can be a significant missed opportunity in affiliate marketing. An email list allows you to communicate directly with your audience, build stronger relationships, and promote your products in a more personalized way.

Pitfall 8: Not Tracking Your Results

Without tracking results, it can be hard to know what's working and what isn't. Utilize analytics tools to monitor performance and use this insight to refine strategies.

By being aware of these potential pitfalls, you can navigate your affiliate marketing journey more successfully and set yourself up for success. In the final chapter we'll offer some final thoughts and advice to make the journey even smoother.

Chapter 10

Final Thoughts and Navigating Your Affiliate Marketing Journey

Affiliate marketing offers tremendous promise but requires consistent effort, careful strategic planning and an attitude of learning and adaptability to achieve results. Before we close this book let's recap some key points and offer final advice.

Key Takeaways

1. Choose Your Niche Carefully: A well-chosen niche aligns with your interests and expertise and has a robust market demand.
2. Select Quality Affiliate Products: Your reputation hinges on the products you endorse. Always choose high-quality, relevant products that offer real value to your audience.
3. Create High-Quality Content: Content is the vehicle for your affiliate promotions. Prioritize value, authenticity, and engagement in your content creation.
4. Understand and Engage Your Audience: The more you know about your audience, the more effectively you can meet their needs and build strong relationships with them.
5. Optimize for SEO: SEO helps your content reach a larger audience by improving its visibility in search engine results.

6. Promote Strategically: Effective promotion involves a mix of strategies, from product reviews and tutorials to email marketing and social media promotion.

7. Diversify and Scale Your Business: As your business grows, explore new affiliate programs, diversify your content and income streams, and leverage tools and resources to become more efficient and effective.

8. Maintain Your Business for Long-Term Success: Keep delivering quality content, engage with your audience, stay updated with industry trends, and continuously analyze and refine your strategies.

9. Avoid Common Pitfalls: From promoting low-quality products to neglecting SEO, be aware of common pitfalls and strive to avoid them.

Final Advice

As you embark on your affiliate marketing journey, remember that success doesn't come overnight. It requires patience, persistence, and a constant desire to learn and improve.

Stay adaptable and be prepared for change. The digital landscape evolves rapidly, and what works today might not work tomorrow. Be ready to learn new strategies, adapt to new trends, and evolve with the industry.

Remember the importance of ethics and transparency in affiliate marketing. Always disclose your affiliate relationships and prioritize your audience's needs over earning commissions. The trust you build with your audience is invaluable and will contribute significantly to your long-term success.

Finally, enjoy the journey. Affiliate marketing can be a fulfilling and rewarding endeavor. It provides an opportunity to share your passion, connect with others, and earn an income doing what you love.

Good luck on your affiliate marketing journey!

Conclusion

The Journey of Affiliate Marketing

Affiliate marketing is an exciting and profitable online business venture that can open doors to financial independence, flexibility and the freedom to work from anywhere in the world. As this guide has demonstrated, affiliate marketing success comes down to understanding your niche, selecting products wisely and carefully promoting them, creating high-quality content; engaging with your target audience and continuously optimizing strategies and plans.

Affiliate marketing should never be seen as a quick way to make quick money; rather it takes hard work, patience, and perseverance - an investment which may start off slow but eventually can yield substantial rewards over time. Successful affiliate marketers recognize the value in providing genuine value to their audience while remaining transparent and honest in all transactions and being willing to adapt in response to changes and learn along with them.

Affiliate marketing is only the start. Once you've mastered its fundamentals, you can move beyond affiliate marketing into creating products of your own or offering consulting services as well as exploring other forms of online promotion.

Remember, in the world of online business, change is the only constant. What worked yesterday may not work tomorrow. Stay updated with industry trends, be willing to learn and adapt, and never lose sight of your audience's needs. Above all, enjoy the journey and the process of building something of your own.

Thank you for choosing this book as your guide in your affiliate marketing journey. Here's to your success!

www.ingramcontent.com/pod-product-compliance
Lightning Source LLC
Chambersburg PA
CBHW080817220526
45466CB00011BB/3592